How Things Work

Text: Sharon Dalgleish
Consultant: Richard Wood, Curator, Powerhouse Museum, Sydney

This edition first published 2003 by
MASON CREST PUBLISHERS INC.
370 Reed Road
Broomall, PA 19008

© Weldon Owen Inc.
Conceived and produced by
Weldon Owen Pty Limited

Library of Congress Cataloging-in-Publication Data
on file at the Library of Congress
ISBN: 1-59084-192-1

Printed in Singapore.
1 2 3 4 5 6 7 8 9 06 05 04 03

CONTENTS

Around the House

Cooking dinner has become easier. Today, microwave ovens use microwaves to cook food quickly. A microwave is a powerful radio wave with a short wavelength. In a normal oven, it takes a long time for the heat to reach the inside of the food and cook it. In a microwave oven, the waves heat the inside of the food at the same time as the outside.

Did You Know?

Most food contains water molecules. When water molecules are hit by microwaves, they vibrate quickly. This vibration makes them heat up, and this heat cooks the food.

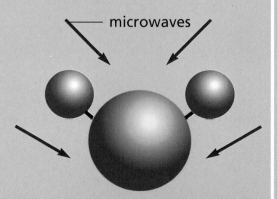

microwaves

Microwaves make the water molecules vibrate.

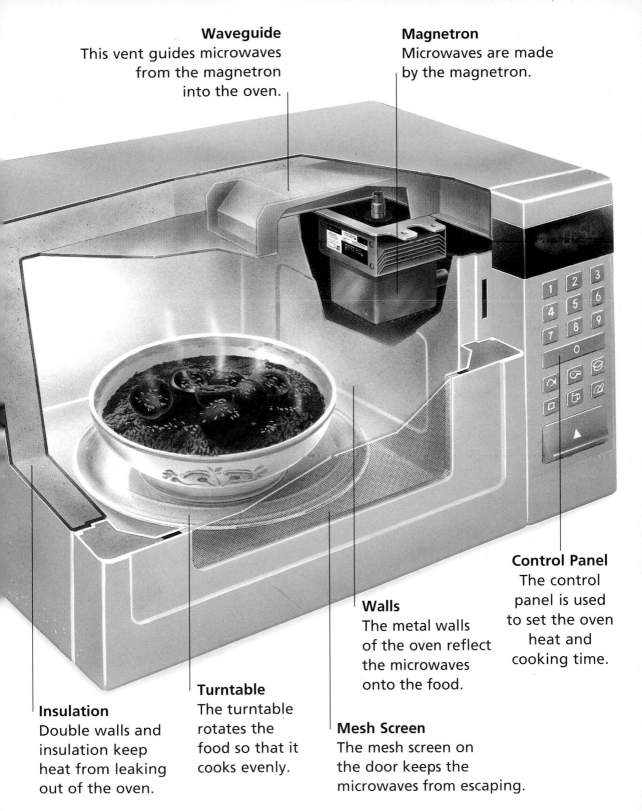

Waveguide
This vent guides microwaves from the magnetron into the oven.

Magnetron
Microwaves are made by the magnetron.

Control Panel
The control panel is used to set the oven heat and cooking time.

Walls
The metal walls of the oven reflect the microwaves onto the food.

Insulation
Double walls and insulation keep heat from leaking out of the oven.

Turntable
The turntable rotates the food so that it cooks evenly.

Mesh Screen
The mesh screen on the door keeps the microwaves from escaping.

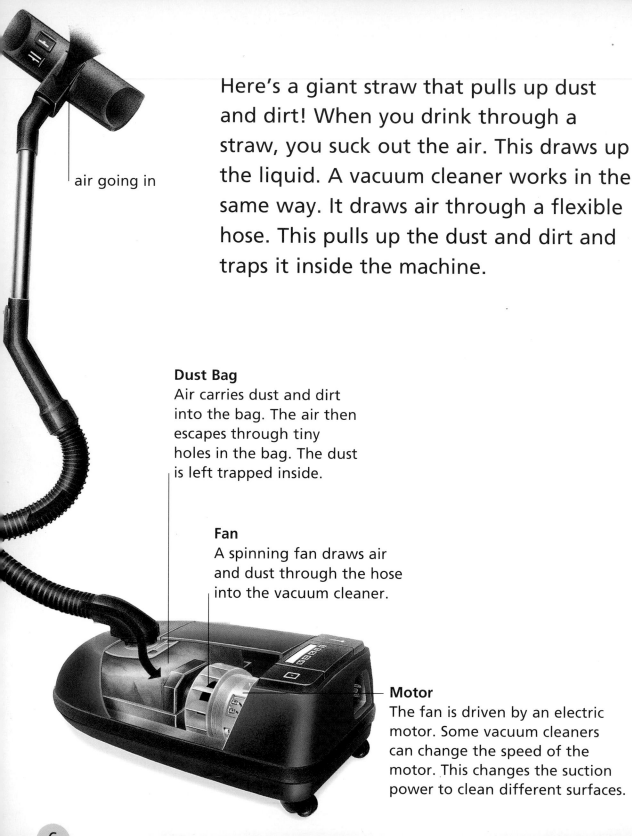

air going in

Here's a giant straw that pulls up dust and dirt! When you drink through a straw, you suck out the air. This draws up the liquid. A vacuum cleaner works in the same way. It draws air through a flexible hose. This pulls up the dust and dirt and traps it inside the machine.

Dust Bag
Air carries dust and dirt into the bag. The air then escapes through tiny holes in the bag. The dust is left trapped inside.

Fan
A spinning fan draws air and dust through the hose into the vacuum cleaner.

Motor
The fan is driven by an electric motor. Some vacuum cleaners can change the speed of the motor. This changes the suction power to clean different surfaces.

DID YOU KNOW?

The first refrigerators used dangerous liquids to cool the air inside. After the 1930s a new substance was used. It wasn't dangerous but it was later found to damage ozone in the Earth's atmosphere. In 1991, an environmentally friendly refrigerator was invented.

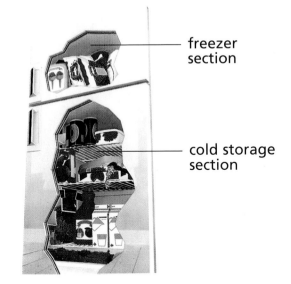

freezer section

cold storage section

A LOOK INSIDE

When the handle on a toilet is pressed, water rushes out of the tank. The float falls and opens a water valve to refill the tank. As the water level rises, the float rises and closes the valve again.

valve

float

tank

water flow

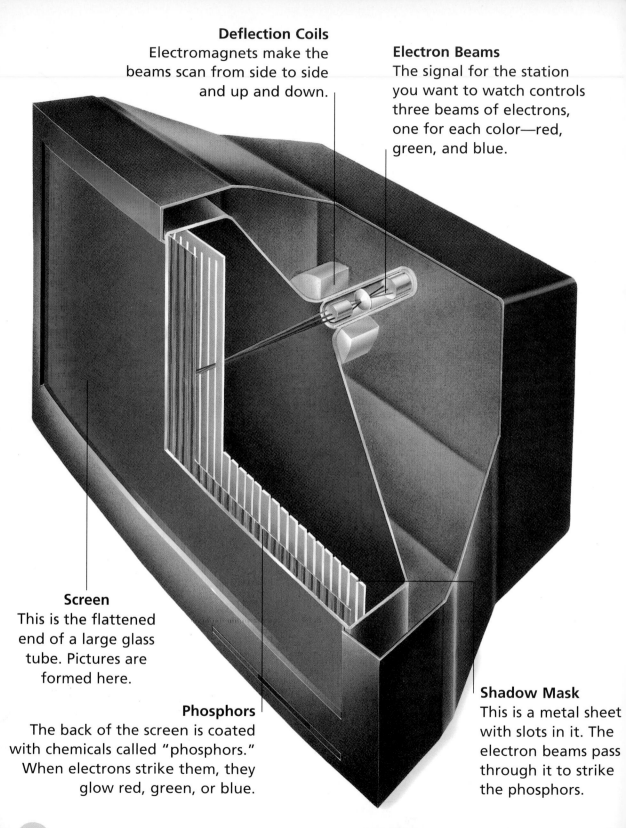

Deflection Coils
Electromagnets make the beams scan from side to side and up and down.

Electron Beams
The signal for the station you want to watch controls three beams of electrons, one for each color—red, green, and blue.

Screen
This is the flattened end of a large glass tube. Pictures are formed here.

Phosphors
The back of the screen is coated with chemicals called "phosphors." When electrons strike them, they glow red, green, or blue.

Shadow Mask
This is a metal sheet with slots in it. The electron beams pass through it to strike the phosphors.

TELEVISIONS

Just like the movies, television plays a trick on your eyes. A television set picks up a signal sent by radio waves or underground cables from a television station. This signal controls a beam that makes a spot glow on the back of the screen. The beam moves the spot from side to side and up and down to build up a picture. The spot moves so quickly that you think the whole screen is glowing at the same time. The pictures flick by quickly one after the other so that you think it is one moving picture.

MAKING COLORS

How can only three colors make a television picture with all the colors of the rainbow? Try this and see.

1 Put a piece of red cellophane over one flashlight, blue over another, and green over a third.

2 In a dark room, ask a friend to help shine the three flashlights on the same spot. Now shine two colors at a time. What colors can you make?

CAMERAS

Smile! As quick as a flash your photograph has been snapped. It was very different in 1826 when the first photograph was taken. That one photograph took eight hours! Today, there are many different film cameras—some simple and some complex. They all work by letting light fall on the film inside.

HOW A CAMERA SEES

When the shutter release button is pressed, the shutter opens and lets light in through the lens. The lens focuses the light onto the film. A chemical on the film captures the image.

DID YOU KNOW?

The roll-film camera was invented in 1888 by George Eastman. This model was called a box "brownie." In 1900 it sold for 50 cents, and that included film!

Winder
Turning the winder moves a new piece of film behind the shutter.

Shutter Release Button
This button is pressed to take a photograph.

Viewfinder
The photographer looks through the viewfinder to see the picture the camera will take.

Film
A plate holds the film behind the shutter and keeps it flat.

Shutter
The shutter opens and closes to let light fall on the film.

Lens System
A number of lenses work together to form a clear, sharp image.

Video Drum
Small electromagnets on the video drum transfer the electrical signals into a magnetic pattern on the video tape.

Video Cassette
The machine opens a flap on the front edge of the cassette, pulls out a loop of tape and wraps it around the video drum.

VCRs and Video Cameras

Video cameras work by dividing a picture into hundreds of lines and scanning the line to work out the color and brightness. This is repeated about 25 times every second, creating a series of pictures that blend to look like a single moving picture. The information in the lines is sent as electrical signals, which are transmitted to your home by radio waves and picked up by an antenna. A video cassette recorder can store the electrical signals from the antenna magnetically on video tape.

DID YOU KNOW?

When a button on the remote control is pressed, it sends a code of invisible infrared pulses to the VCR or television. The VCR or television detects the code and changes the volume or channel.

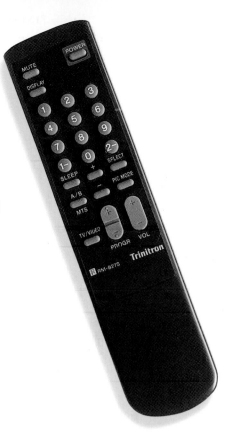

VIDEO CAMERA

When the video camera was invented in 1931, it was bigger than a person. It could produce and send pictures but not record them. In 1981 a video camera that could record as well was invented. It was small enough to be held by hand.

LASERS

One hundred years ago, a beam of light that could cut through bricks was just a science-fiction story. Today, a laser beam so strong it can cut through metal is a reality. Laser light is different from light from an ordinary lightbulb. Light beams from a lightbulb have no direction and a range of wavelengths. Light beams from a laser are parallel and have even wavelengths. The power from a lightbulb is 100 watts. The power from a laser is 10 billion watts.

DID YOU KNOW?

A compact disc player uses light made by a laser. A lens focuses the beam of light onto the disc, which stores sound as tiny holes. The light bounces off these holes and the reflection is changed into electricity and converted to sound.

laser

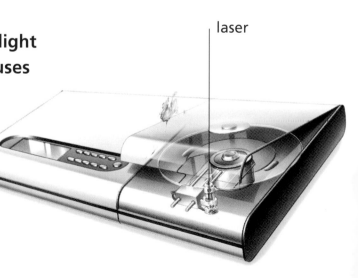

DIFFERENT WAVES

Light from a laser can be focused by a lens. Light from a bulb cannot be focused.

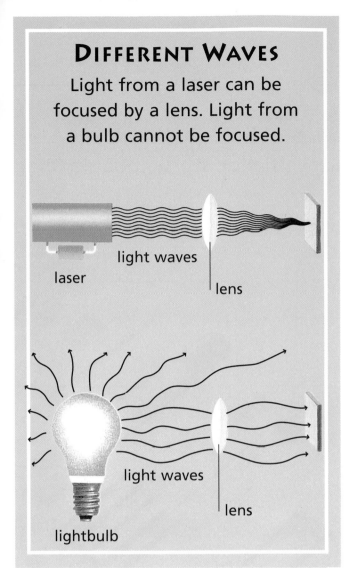

light waves

laser

lens

light waves

lens

lightbulb

HEALING LIGHT

Different types of lasers have different wavelengths. Doctors use them for different things. The first laser in the diagram is used to cut tissue. The second laser is absorbed by blood and can stop bleeding. The third laser is used for deep treatment.

BAR CODE SCANNER

As the laser beam scans the bar code, a sensor in the handset picks up the reflection. It makes electrical pulses in the same pattern as the black code lines. A computer translates the code and identifies the product.

FAX MACHINES

A fax machine can send a written message or picture anywhere in the world in seconds. It changes the information on the paper into electrical signals. These signals are changed into sounds, which are sent along telephone lines.

Print Head
When a message is received, a row of lights flash on and off. Black powder sticks to the drum wherever this light strikes it.

Numerical Keypad
These keys are used to dial telephone numbers.

paper storage tray

Image Scanner
When you send a message, the scanner produces an electrical signal, which is changed into sounds and sent down a telephone line. Another fax machine changes the sounds back into a printed copy.

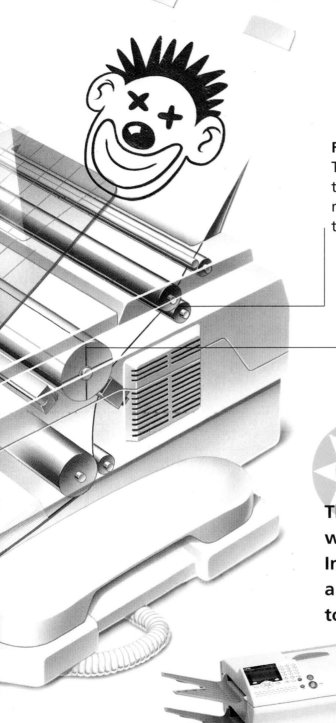

Fuser Unit
The paper leaves the machine through a pair of rollers. They melt the black powder from the drum to the paper.

Drum
The drum turns around and attracts black powder.

DID YOU KNOW?

The first fax machine was invented around 1900. In 1907 a German scientist sent a photograph by telephone line to England. But no one realized what a useful invention this was until 70 years later.

Monitor
This displays
information
from the
computer. It
looks like
a small
television
screen.

Microprocessor
The microprocessor is the
master chip that controls
the computer. It can
have several hundred
thousand parts.

Speakers
These play music,
sound effects, or speech.

CD-ROM Drive
This copies information from a CD-ROM onto
the computer. It can't record information
onto the CD-ROM. "CD-ROM" stands for
Compact Disc Read-Only Memory.

COMPUTERS

Inside a computer are microscopic electronic circuits built into silicon chips. These hard-working chips can store huge amounts of information. They can also carry out instructions very quickly to do different jobs—from writing, to calculating, to playing games.

FLOPPY DISK

Information is stored as magnetic patterns on a thin disk. A stiff plastic case protects the floppy disk.

Mouse
This controls a pointer on the screen.

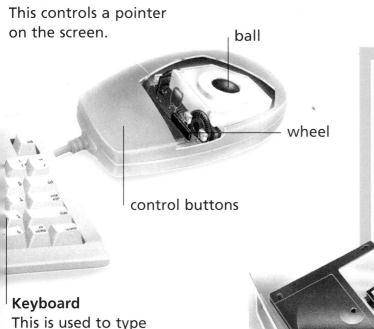

ball

wheel

control buttons

Keyboard
This is used to type information into the computer.

DISK DRIVE

The floppy disk drive works like a tape recorder. It copies information from the computer onto the floppy disk or from the floppy disk onto the computer.

TELEPHONES

A telephone changes the sound of a voice
into an electrical signal that is sent along a
cable. The path the signal takes along the
cable depends on the number dialed.
Another telephone then changes the signal
back into sound.

Coil
The electrical signal coming through
the cable passes through a coil and
creates a weak magnetic field.

Magnet
The magnet attracts or repels
the coil and makes it vibrate.

Diaphragm
The vibrating coil causes the diaphragm
to vibrate and make a sound.

Diaphragm
The speaker's voice makes
the diaphragm vibrate.

Coil
The vibrating diaphragm makes the coil
vibrate next to a magnet. This causes an
electric current that is sent along the cable.

antenna

earpiece

MOBILE PHONE

Mobile phones don't need cables. The calls travel on radio waves. Every mobile telephone has its own radio transmitter and receiver.

battery

display

microphone

DID YOU KNOW?

keypad

You can make a string telephone by joining two cans with a long length of string. Pull the string tight and talk into one can. A friend at the other end can hear you.

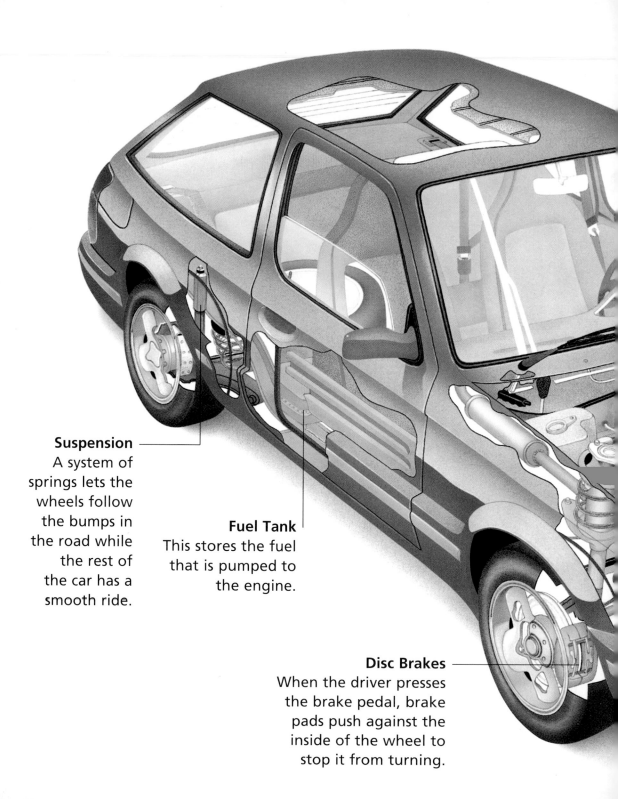

Suspension
A system of springs lets the wheels follow the bumps in the road while the rest of the car has a smooth ride.

Fuel Tank
This stores the fuel that is pumped to the engine.

Disc Brakes
When the driver presses the brake pedal, brake pads push against the inside of the wheel to stop it from turning.

CARS

Cars have a number of different systems that all work together. The fuel system supplies fuel to the engine. The transmission system transmits the power from the engine to the wheels. The suspension system gives the passengers a smooth ride. Finally, the braking system stops the car safely.

Battery
The battery starts the engine.

Radiator and Fan
Water is pumped through the radiator and cooled by a fan. This keeps the engine from getting too hot.

Distributor
This sends electrical sparks to light the fuel.

Engine
The engine burns fuel to make power to turn the wheels.

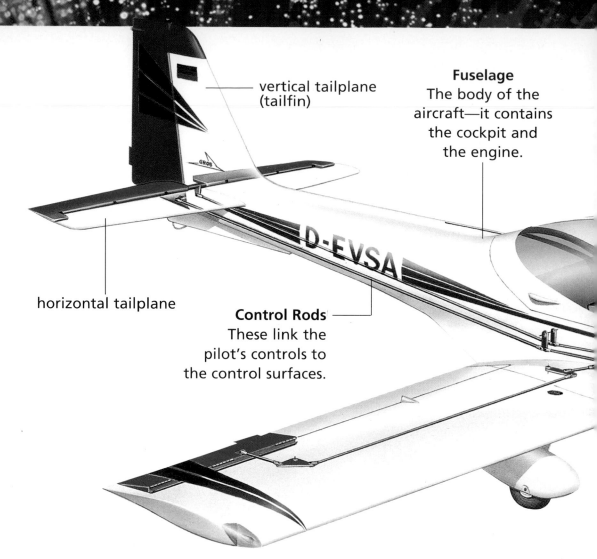

vertical tailplane
(tailfin)

Fuselage
The body of the
aircraft—it contains
the cockpit and
the engine.

horizontal tailplane

Control Rods
These link the
pilot's controls to
the control surfaces.

AIRPLANES

Airplanes look so heavy that they couldn't possibly fly, yet
they can. This is because air travels faster over the curved
top of the wings than across the flat bottom. The difference
in air pressure pulls the wings upward. To make the plane
turn, climb, or dive the pilot moves panels in the wings and
tail, which are called "control surfaces."

Control Column
This moves to work the control surfaces on the wings and tailplanes.

Propeller
The engine turns the blades on the propeller. This pulls air over the aircraft and it moves forward.

Rudder Pedals
These control the rudder and the brakes.

STRANGE BUT TRUE
Radar sends out pulses of radio waves. These bounce off any large metal objects in their path. Some travel back to the radar dish. The time this takes is measured and used to calculate the exact distance to the plane.

HOT AIR BALLOONS

Hot air balloons work because they are filled with hot air. Hot air is lighter than cold air so when the air inside the balloon is heated, the balloon lifts. This air can get very hot. The gas burners used to heat it are powerful enough to heat 120 houses. Balloonists use the air to control their height—when the hot air is replaced by cooler, heavier air, the balloon comes down again. However, they have little control over their direction. They have to travel where the wind takes them.

DID YOU KNOW?

In 1783 the first hot air balloon was made from paper and cloth and held together with buttons. Its passengers were a sheep, a duck, and a rooster. Two months later, the first human passengers flew through the sky.

Envelope
This is made of nylon that doesn't rip.

parachute vent

Burners
Two gas burners blast heat into the balloon.

Basket
Most baskets are made of woven willow.

ripcord

UP, UP, AND AWAY

To make the balloon rise, balloonists heat the air in the balloon. To lower the balloon, they turn the gas down so the air cools, or pull the ripcord to let hot air escape from the vent.

HELICOPTERS

A helicopter has a set of spinning wings called a rotor. The pilot can tilt the rotor forward to fly the helicopter forward, backward to fly backward, or sideways to fly sideways. To hover in one place, the pilot has to operate all the controls at once. It's like trying to pat your head and rub your stomach while balancing on a basketball!

Main Rotor
This lifts the helicopter straight up by screwing up into the air—like a screw going into a piece of wood.

Cyclic Control
This tilts the whole rotor to change direction.

Collective Control
This changes the angle of the rotor blades. To go up, the pilot tilts the blades at a steep angle.

Rudder Pedals
These are linked to the small tail rotor. The pilot uses them to hold the helicopter in a straight line.

Tail Rotor
This keeps the helicopter from spinning in the opposite direction to the main rotor.

MAKE A HELICOPTER

What you need
- 1 piece of cardboard
- pencil
- scissors
- ruler
- 1 paper clip

Steps one and two

1 Use a pencil and ruler to copy the pattern at right onto a piece of cardboard.

2 Cut along the line A to B.

3 Fold the rotor along the dotted lines.

4 Attach a paper clip and launch your helicopter into the air.

Steps three and four

Glossary

antenna A device that receives or transmits radio waves.

electromagnetic wave A wave of energy made of vibrating electric and magnetic fields.

electronic circuits The pathways and connections followed by electrons to control computers and many modern appliances.

electrons Tiny particles with negative electric charges. Electrons moving in the same direction form an electric current.

light Electromagnetic waves that the human eye can see.

molecules A group of atoms linked together to make a substance, such as water.

ozone A colorless gas that filters out harmful ultraviolet radiation from the Sun high in the Earth's atmosphere.

radio waves Invisible electromagnetic waves that carry information, such as the human voice.

valve A device that starts or stops the flow of a gas or a liquid.

INDEX

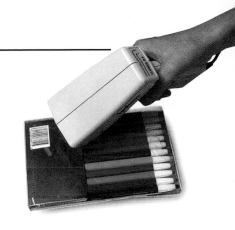

PICTURE AND ILLUSTRATION CREDITS

BOOKS IN THIS SERIES